People Not

Reflections on Transgender Experience

Andrew Bunt

Assistant Pastor, King's Church Hastings and Bexhill,

Associate at Living Out

GROVE BOOKS LIMITED

RIDLEY HALL RD CAMBRIDGE CB3 9HU

Contents

Acknowledgments

My thanks to those who read and gave feedback on earlier drafts of this booklet, especially the Grove Pastoral Series Editorial Group, and to all who have discussed this topic with me and encouraged me in this project.

Special thanks to those who have spoken with me for whom the experiences discussed in this book are real-life. I am grateful for your honesty and wisdom.

I pray that this small booklet will play its part in shaping churches where those who identify as transgender or who experience gender dysphoria can experience the love and the hope that Jesus offers us all.

First Impression June 2021
ISSN 0144-171X
ISBN 978 1 78827 126 4

1 Introduction

There was a time in my childhood when I thought I was a girl. Although externally my body seemed to suggest I was a boy, and everyone else seemed to believe I was a boy, I thought that really, I must be a girl. At school, I always wanted to be with the girls. While almost all the other boys would be playing football, I was with the girls, trying (and failing) to do handstands. My best friends were always girls. I just did not feel comfortable with the boys.

One of my most vivid memories is the day I was suddenly struck by the fear that I might become pregnant. (Clearly this was before I knew how these things work!) If that happened, there would be no hiding my big secret. I concluded that I would not be able to get married and would just have to remain living with my parents forever.

As I grew up and went through my teenage years, the feeling that I might be a girl trapped in a boy's body faded away, but I continued to be uncomfortable with my masculinity. I still preferred the company of girls and felt actively uncomfortable in all-male contexts. Stag dos were my worst nightmare—I would usually just find a way to avoid them—but I secretly harboured a desire that one of my female friends would invite me to their hen do. I wanted to be one of the girls. And when a man said something that I and my female friends thought objectionable, I would say, 'He would say that. He's a man.' Clearly, he was in a group that I felt I was not.

This experience of discomfort with my gender identity has been fairly mild compared to the experiences of some. Some children experience much greater distress over their gender than I did in childhood, and for some people, these strong feelings continue through adolescence and into adulthood. In other, rarer cases, the discomfort can suddenly appear later in life. For some, the tension between the external characteristics of the body and the internal feelings of identity, or the clash between their community's and their own perception of themselves, is deeply distressing and painful, sometimes even making just living feel almost impossible.

Understanding Transgender

Transgender is a complex concept. In part this complexity is because the term can be used to cover a broad range of experiences. Stonewall, a prominent LGBT rights charity, defines transgender as:

> An umbrella term to describe people whose gender is not the same as, or does not sit comfortably with, the sex they were assigned at birth.[1]

This definition draws on two prior concepts:

> *Gender* is (in this context) an individual's personal, internal sense of being a man or a woman. This is sometimes referred to as 'gender identity' or 'experienced gender.'
>
> *Sex* is the identification as male or female based on physical anatomy (that is, chromosomes, gonads, genitals and hormones). Some who do not see these elements of anatomy as determinative prefer the terms 'sex assigned at birth' or 'assigned sex.'

To be transgender, then, is to experience a tension or conflict between an identity suggested by certain elements of the physical anatomy one is born with (sex) and one's internal sense of self (gender).

Another key term is 'gender dysphoria,' the medical diagnosis made when someone experiences considerable distress because of transgender experience.

Many different experiences and identities can be placed under the broad term 'transgender' (for example nonbinary, genderqueer or genderfluid), and there is debate over whether one must experience gender dysphoria in order to be able to identify as transgender. In this booklet, I will focus primarily on how Christians can best respond to those whose sex and gender are in conflict with one another and who experience gender dysphoria, although much of what I will say will also be applicable to other related experiences and identities.[2]

At this point, it is worth noting the distinction between transgender and intersex. People with intersex conditions are born with bodily characteristics which exhibit differences from the expected pattern for either male or female. Intersex is, therefore, somewhat different from transgender, and it is often unhelpful to seek to address the two together. Because of limitations of space, I will only address transgender in this booklet.

Transgender Debates

Transgender experience and gender dysphoria have given rise to many debates.

The key debate is on how transgender experience and, especially, the pain of gender dysphoria should be handled. Can the conflict between sex and gender be reconciled, and, if so, which one should change? Do we seek to help people change their internal sense of gender so that it matches their sex? Or do we help people change their bodies so that they more closely reflect the sex that matches their gender? In many circles, the former approach has been deemed ineffective and even harmful.[3] The latter approach is now widely accepted and practised, though it is not without its critics. This process, known as transitioning, can start with social transitioning in which an individual adopts a name, pronouns and external presentation which matches their gender, and can be followed by legal transitioning (obtaining a Gender Recognition Certificate and new birth certificate) and medical transitioning (which may include hormone treatment and surgery).

How should the pain of gender dysphoria be handled?

The debate is most active when it comes to the treatment of children with gender dysphoria. While some campaign for early transitioning—which has sometimes been facilitated by medical professionals—there is an increasing pushback against this approach from medical professionals, parents and detransitioners (those who transitioned, often at a young age, but have since returned to live in line with their sex).

Other debates have tended to focus around some of the practical implications of transitioning. Should people be able to use the sex-segregated spaces, such as public toilets and changing rooms, of the gender they identify with? Which prisons should transgender prisoners be sent to? Can trans people compete in sports competitions for those of the gender with which they identify? And which pronouns (those little words like 'he' and 'she') should be used for transgender people?

People Not Pronouns

For many Christians, these public debates are the only real insight we have into the topic. Observing from a distance, transgender can easily become an issue of public toilets, prisons and pronouns, a political issue driven by activists.

These debates are important, and there is a role for Christians to play in them if we are willing to engage thoughtfully and sensitively, but before we get to the debates, we should engage with the people. Behind the debates, behind the news stories, behind (and often not amongst) the activists are real people, people created by God and loved by God, who are wrestling with their sense of self and are often suffering great pain and distress in the process. A truly Christian response to transgender must start by engaging with those who are personally affected. We must start from the realization that this is not primarily a topic about public toilets, prisons or pronouns. It is about people.

A Christian Response

The focus of this booklet will be on how we as Christians should respond to people who identify as transgender or who experience gender dysphoria. I will explore three elements of a response: a heart response, a head response and a hope response. There are many practical questions that I will not have space to discuss, but the principles outlined here will give each of us a basis from which to think through such questions.

2 A Heart Response

I'm transgender. I'm looking for a church. Can I come to yours?

Biologically male, Miya had experienced gender dysphoria from around the age of five.[4] As a child, they genuinely thought they would one day wake up with a girl's body. When Miya came out to their church as transgender, they were told that not only were they going to hell but by attending the church they were forcing everyone there into sin and jeopardizing each person's salvation. Miya was told to leave. After a while, Miya started to contact other churches to ask this question. Most churches just ignored the messages.

Jordan is biologically female, but from the age of four has experienced acute gender dysphoria. A number of years ago, they were part of a church where the pastor preached on transgender and said that anyone who is trans is destined to burn in hell. A few years later, Jordan summoned the courage to share about their experience of gender dysphoria with a pastor. After bravely opening up about the pain and confusion of their experience, Jordan was promptly thrown out of the pastor's office through a side door and told never to come back.

Sadly, Miya's and Jordan's experiences are not unique. Many transgender people have experienced Christians as those who make them feel ashamed or who simply reject them. Churches are not seen as safe spaces for those who identify as transgender. But as Christians, we should be known as the most honouring and welcoming of people, and churches should be known as the most safe of places.

It is possible to have the right theology—the head response—without having the right heart. If we know God's truth but we fail to communicate it with his heart, we are not really responding like him, and if we are not responding like him, we are not making a truly Christian response. We must, therefore, start with a heart response.

The Heart of Jesus

One of the best ways to understand God's heart is to look at the example of Jesus. Jesus is God come to Earth as a man, and so when we see him relating to people, we get an insight into the heart of God.

Many people think that God hates transgender people. As both Miya and Jordan found, the assumption is often that there is no place among the people of God for those with gender dysphoria. But when we look to the example of Jesus, we find that he never just hates anyone. Jesus did sometimes become deeply frustrated, perhaps even righteously angry, but when he did, this feeling was towards the hypocritical religious leaders. Jesus' anger was against those who teach one thing but do another, those who judge others but fail to apply the same judgment to themselves. His anger was directed against those who fail to love others and who seem only to love themselves. But even in these cases, there is no suggestion that Jesus does not love them.

That is pretty amazing in itself. But what is most amazing about the example of Jesus is how he treats those whom everyone assumed God would hate. In Jesus' day, this was the tax collectors, prostitutes and lepers, those who were rejected and even hated by the religious elite. But Jesus does not hate them and he does not reject them. Jesus talks to them (Luke 7.48), eats with them (Luke 5.29–30) and stays with them (Luke 19.5). Jesus loves them. We find that the very people the religious elite assumed God would hate are those whom Jesus is most eager to befriend and to love.

When we look at Jesus we see that he loved, and he loved even those whom others assumed he should hate. Where there was sin, he never condoned it. He never separated God's truth and God's love, but he knew that he could not truly express God's truth if he did not also express God's heart.

Jesus reveals that in the heart of God is a deep love for every person he has created, and a deep desire for them to find fullness of life in him. So, when we look at Jesus, we see that God loves transgender people. If you are trans, do not believe the lie that God hates you. If you know people who are trans, do not believe the lie that God hates them. God loves you if you are trans. God loves your friend if they are trans.

God's heart towards those who are transgender is love

If God's heart towards those who are transgender is love, our heart should be the same. If we find that our default response is something other than love—perhaps disgust or anger—we must examine why this is, and allow the example of Jesus to challenge us and the Holy Spirit to change us.

Jesus was Compassionate

Jesus' example also shows us that he feels great compassion for people with gender dysphoria.

For those of us who have never experienced acute gender dysphoria, it can be hard to imagine what the experience would be like. One transgender author offers an imaginative exercise to help us gain a little insight:

> [I]magine waking up in the morning and having to wear the clothes you associate with the opposite sex. All day long, you must conform to society's ideas of what it means to be a woman or a man…Give yourself a moment to seriously imagine what this would be like—throughout your childhood, day after day as an adult, to feel this uncomfortable, like you were being forced into a gender role that doesn't fit you.[5]

Most people with gender dysphoria acknowledge that it is very difficult to describe. Some talk about looking in a mirror and feeling like the person looking back is not really them. Some cannot even bear to look at themselves in a mirror. For some, the feelings of discomfort with their body are so acute that they contemplate cutting off parts of their body. (One friend has spoken of multiple occasions where they have sat in a hospital car park, thinking of self-mutilating because the pain of dysphoria has become too great.) In some cases, dysphoria is fairly constant and inescapable, while for others it varies in strength over time.

How would Jesus respond to such experiences? How should we, as his followers, respond?

With compassion. In the gospels, when Jesus encounters suffering, whether physical or psychological, he responds with compassion (*eg* Matt 9.36; 15.32; 20.34; Mark 6.34; 8.2; Luke 7.13). The verb used in these verses (*splanchnizomai*) is derived from a noun (*splanchnon*) used for a person's innards, the parts of the body which were thought to be the seat of the emotions. It speaks of a deep, gut feeling, of being moved deeply.

One of the most striking examples of Jesus' compassion comes in Matt 14.13–14. Having heard news of John the Baptist's death, Jesus gets in a boat to withdraw to be alone in a quiet place, but when the boat reaches the shore, the people had already gathered in a crowd. Many of us would find it easy to become frustrated at this point. But Jesus does not. Even in this context, he sees the crowd, he sees that many are suffering, and he has compassion on them. For Jesus, compassion was the natural response to suffering.

For Jesus, compassion was the natural response to suffering

And this is an attitude which followers of Jesus are meant to embody, even towards those whom others might exclude and judge. In the Parable of the Good Samaritan, the Samaritan sees the suffering of the man who has been attacked and has compassion on him (Luke 10.33). When the lawyer who had prompted Jesus to tell the story identifies the Samaritan as the true neighbour, it is this element of compassion which is stressed. The true neighbour is 'The one who showed him mercy' (Luke 10.37).[6] Christians are meant to embody the compassion of Jesus.

As Christians, we are uniquely equipped to express the compassion of God, and from that place of compassion to communicate comfort to others. In the blessing which opens 2 Corinthians, Paul describes God as 'the Father of compassion and God of all comfort' (1.3 NIV). Compassion has its source in God, and, as Paul goes on to explain, God 'comforts us in all our troubles, so that we can comfort those in any trouble with the comfort we ourselves receive from God' (1.4 NIV). Both our compassion, and the comfort it leads us to bring, flow from God himself.

As Christians, we are uniquely equipped to express the compassion of God

When we encounter the reality of gender dysphoria and the pain that it brings, our hearts should be moved with compassion. How can we grow in compassion? By seeing the suffering. Jesus' compassion was a response to the suffering he could see around him. The same should be true for us.

Love and Compassion in Action

What does it look like to express this love and compassion in action? How do we put this into practice?

The first step is actually to cultivate our hearts so that love and compassion become our default response. We do this by becoming more like Jesus, allowing him to shape us as we mature in him. This is something we should be active in, pursuing maturity through spiritual disciplines and committed participation in a local church.

Our hearts will also be shaped as we get to know transgender people and those who experience gender dysphoria. As we begin to connect with the real people behind the debates, our hearts can grow in love for each individual and in compassion for those who are suffering. Some of us will have the privilege of doing this in the context of relationship with those who are personally affected by the topic. If this opportunity is not immediately available to us, we can gain some level of insight through reading or watching the stories of transgender people. In doing this, we might encounter some views with which we do not agree and do not believe are God's best for the individuals involved, but that should not stop us from seeing through this to seek to better understand the real people whose stories we are hearing.

Love and compassion are expressed in listening before we talk. This is a way to affirm people's dignity and a way to honour them as individuals, whose experiences and feelings matter. This applies as much on the broader level of the cultural conversation as it does in our friendships with transgender people. Just as our friendships should be characterized by a humble listening, so also our engagement in the broader cultural conversation should start with careful listening. We should seek to understand fully before we speak. We should seek to see the real people and respond in a way which puts them first. As so often in life, listening is the start of loving.

Love and compassion are expressed in listening before we talk

We also express love and compassion through our speaking. Words are incredibly powerful. They can do great good and great harm. There is absolutely no place for joking about gender identity or transgender experience among Christians. To make jokes about the real-life experience and suffering of others does not express the heart of Jesus. We should be sure to talk about transgender people in the way we would want others to talk about us or our family or close friends, recognizing their full dignity as those created in the image of God.

We should also be careful when we are commenting on the wider cultural debates. When posting on social media, making public statements or even just talking in personal conversation, we should always have real people in mind. How would this make them feel? What would it make them believe God thinks and feels about them? Is this expressing the heart of God?

Love and compassion are also expressed through a wholehearted welcome. As we will see, some transgender people will make choices about the way they respond to and express their experience which we may believe are not in keeping with God's desire for them. But in the example of Jesus, we see that these people are exactly those to whom God is so keen to reach out and to welcome in.

It is possible truly to love and welcome those with whom we disagree. Jesus proves that to be true, even if our culture cannot believe it. As followers of Jesus, we can embody his way by welcoming all so that they can experience the love and welcome of God through us.

The right heart response must be the starting point for a Christian response to transgender. A heart attitude of love and compassion must underpin both the other elements (which we will explore in chapters three and four) of a Christian response.

Discussion Questions

- How can you, as an individual, grow in your love and compassion for transgender people?
- How can your church make sure it is a safe place for transgender people?

A Head Response

3

As we turn to consider a head response—how we should think about transgender—we face some of the most difficult questions: are some people born in the wrong body? Should there even be a binary of man and woman? And, perhaps most importantly, should people who experience gender dysphoria transition to live in line with their experienced gender rather than their sex?

These are huge, complex questions, but central to them all—and to the whole topic of transgender—is the issue of identity. Transgender experience is often presented as people finding their true identity. It is presented as an answer to the question, 'Who am I?'

'Who am I?' is a really important question to ask. It is a very human question. We all need to know who we really are. We all need an identity which is solid, stable and life-giving. And it is by learning who we really are and embracing that identity that we are able to experience fullness of life.

When it comes to the topic of transgender, many people assume that identity is found in experienced gender, in how we feel internally. They therefore conclude that for those whose gender is in conflict with their sex, transitioning to live in line with experienced gender will be the route to satisfaction.

The problem with this approach is that it answers the question 'Who am I?' without first asking the important question, 'How do I find who I am?'

Finding Identity

For many people in the modern West, the answer to this question is internal identity: you look inside yourself at your feelings and desires, and there you find the real you. This true self, discovered within, is unaffected by anything external such as our body or community. Therefore, our feelings and desires should be expressed and lived out to experience our best life. Younger westerners, in particular, are constantly being taught this understanding through popular media.

To transition is to embrace an internal identity

This is the form of identity which underpins a pro-transitioning approach to gender dysphoria. To transition is to embrace an internal identity.

This internal identity narrative can often be seen quite explicitly in coming out stories. One example comes from an interview with Caitlyn Jenner, one of the most famous transgender celebrities. Asked how she decided that 2015 was the right time to come out, Jenner replied, 'I had a lot of conversations… and kind of came to a revelation, that maybe I should be honest with myself about *who I am* and let that person—*this woman who has lived inside me for my entire life*—finally have an opportunity to live.'[7] Jenner clearly combines the language of identity ('who I am') with ideas about the internal ('has lived inside me'). For Jenner, coming out and transitioning was embracing an internal identity that had long been trapped in her body.

This response to transgender is based on internal identity. How do I find who I am? I look inside myself at my feelings and desires. They reveal the real me.

But there are some big problems with internal identity. First, it is *unstable*. An internal identity is based on our feelings and desires, but we all know that these can change. They cannot provide a solid, stable identity. Internal identity is also *ambiguous*. Our feelings and desires can easily conflict. What if we deeply desire two things which cannot be reconciled. Which do we embrace to find our true self? And ultimately, internal identity is *inconsistent*. We all agree that there are desires we might experience which we would not embrace as our identity. If, for example, someone had a strong desire to kill lots of people, we would not encourage them to embrace that desire as their true self, or to express it in order to experience their best life. In reality, no one really believes in the narrative of internal identity; rather, we pick and choose the desires which are approved by our society and we build our identity on those.

Internal identity is inconsistent

A final problem with internal identity is simply that there is no authority behind the choice to prioritize the internal. If there is a conflict between the external body and the internal self, why should we prioritize the internal? When experienced gender and sex conflict, why should we prioritize gender?

If internal identity does not work, we need another way of finding or forming our identity. Some people replace the internal with the external, building an identity on what they do, how good they are, and on what (they think) others think of them. But this is just as problematic. What happens if you can no longer do what you once did? What happens if you make a big mistake and no longer seem so good to others? And what happens if people just change their opinion of you? There is no stability in an external identity. We need a better answer.

The Gift of Divine Identity

The better answer is in divine identity: identity given to us by God. Only such an identity can be truly static, stable and life-giving.

As creatures, we are meant to get our identity from God. If he made us, that makes complete sense.

The Bible tells us that for all humans a key part of our identity is being in the image of God (Gen 1.26–27). This is an identity which is given to us by God. It is not based on how we feel, what we desire, or what we do; it is based on what God says and how he has created us. It is solid, static, stable and can never change.[8] This identity is important: it speaks of the value and worth of every human life (Gen 9.6; Jas 3.9).

In Genesis 1, the next part of our identity that is mentioned is our identity as either male or female.

> So God created man in his own image,
>   in the image of God he created him;
>   male and female he created them.
>
> Gen 1.27

The creation of humans as male or female is placed in parallel with the creation of humans in the image of God. This tells us several important things.

First, it tells us that both males and females are equally created in the image of God and are completely equal in worth, dignity and the right to life.

Secondly, it tells us that our identity as male or female is given to us by God, just as our identity as those bearing God's image is given to us by him. The parallel structure of Gen 1.27 shows that the image of God and male and female work in the same way. Both are identities given to us by God and spoken over us in creation, and which remain solid, static and unchanged throughout our lives. This means we do not have to act or feel a certain way to be a man or a woman. We are a man or a woman because of how God has made us.

And this given identity can be discerned through the body given to us by God. This is implied in the very next verse. The declaration that humans are created male and female is immediately followed by the blessing to 'Be fruitful and multiply and fill the earth' (Gen 1.28). Creation as male or female naturally flows into a commission to reproduce because it is our body's orientation towards reproduction that identifies us as male or female. Scientists recognize that the reproductive system is the only truly binary part of a creature that can be used to identify biological sex.[9] We receive our God-given identity as male or female through our body.

All of this fits with a biblical view of the body. Internal identity sees the body as, at best, a home for the true self that resides within, or, at worst, an annoying distraction from the reality of the true self. The body is not deemed to be part of the true self. By contrast, the Bible presents humans as embodied beings. It is not that our true self resides in our bodies. Our bodies are part of our true self. They are part of God's good creation.

Living Out Divine Identity

If our identity as either male or female is given to us by God and communicated to us through our bodies, and if embracing our true identity is the route to fullness of life, it makes sense that the Bible consistently expects males to live as men and females to live as women. It also makes sense that any crossing of gender boundaries is viewed negatively in the Bible (*eg* Deut 22.5; 1 Cor 11.3–16).

But what does it mean for males to live as men and for females to live as women? Does it mean that men must be tough, meat-eating and sports-loving, while women should be gentle and enjoy crafts and pretty things? Certainly not! The Bible only gives two clear ways that we are to live out our sexed identities.

First, our sex should be identifiable from our external presentation (Deut 22.5; 1 Cor 11.3–16).[10] Our bodies give us a head start on this (through our secondary sex characteristics), and it is then continued in how we choose to dress and style our hair. Secondly, some Christians believe the Bible teaches that there are different roles for men and women in the context of marriage relationships and in church leadership structures.

Beyond this, there is little clear biblical guidance about what it means to live as a man or as a woman, and yet we often put many additional expectations on men and women. These sorts of gender stereotypes are common both in the culture around us and in the church. In the world around us they are often prominent in the stories of transgender people. One dad interviewed in a documentary about transgender children said that he knew his son was a girl when he saw them run. This is diagnosis by stereotypes. Such stereotypes can be prominent in churches in the things we say, the jokes we make and the events we run.

Many people find that these stereotypes leave them feeling like they are less than a 'proper man' or 'proper woman.' Even for those who do not experience gender dysphoria, this sense of not really fitting in with others of the same sex or of not really making the cut as a man or woman can be a common effect of rigid, unbiblical stereotypes. But as we have already seen, our identity as a man or a woman is given to us by God through our bodies and is unchangeable. We do not have to act a certain way to create or earn that identity. We have received it from God, and now we get to express it in line with our God-given personality and preferences. Divine identity allows us to be *how* we are without affecting *who* we are.

Divine identity allows us to be how we are without affecting who we are

My experience of continued discomfort with my masculinity in adolescence and early adulthood was the result of stereotypes. I had a set idea of what a real man was like, and I very clearly did not fit into that box. I did not make the cut. Recognizing that my identity as a man is something given to me by God, and is unchangeable, helped me to become comfortable in my masculinity. I realized that I am a man because God says I am a man, not because of some ability to live up to a certain set of standards. I am a man and therefore I can live out my identity as a man with the unique personality and preferences that God has given me. This means I do not need to worry about not liking sport, hating aggression and usually finding it easier to develop friendships with women than with men. And it means I can embrace my love of musicals and *Downton Abbey*, and my sometimes flamboyant nature, as none of these things change my identity. I can be how I am, without it changing who I am.

I suspect that many people would be helped if we recognized the given nature of our sexed identity, and avoided unbiblical and unnecessary gender stereotypes.

But what does all of this mean for those who experience more acute gender dysphoria and for those who identify as transgender?

First, it means it is not possible to be born in the wrong body. This idea relies on a separation between the body and the true self which, as we have seen, does not fit the biblical picture of human identity. Our body is part of our true self. It is not possible for it to be in conflict with the truth about us.[11]

It also means that transitioning to live in line with experienced gender is not the right or the best approach when an individual experiences a strong conflict between sex and gender.[12]

This is not an easy thing to say. Every time I say it I can see in my mind's eye the faces of those who live with the pain of gender dysphoria. I think of those who cannot look at themselves in a mirror. I think of young people who have said that life will not be bearable if they have to remain living in line with their sex. I think of adults who have said that they wake each morning not knowing whether they will be able to get through the day still winning the internal battle against the urge to cut their own body. I think of the pain, the strain, the tears and the anguish.

Sometimes it all makes me wish the answer was different. But I continue to believe that what God says about our sex and gender is right and good. And this is not just blind obedience—it is trust. Everything we know about the God revealed in Jesus suggests that he is supremely trustworthy on matters such as this. In a way I can never be, he is perfectly wise and perfectly good, and so I know that what he says is always wise and always good. I know that he can be trusted.

What God says about our sex and gender is right and good

It should be noted, however, that the application of this truth in the life of a transgender person who wants to follow Jesus will likely not be instantaneous. For all of us, discipleship is a journey of growing in obedience. The moment of conversion requires genuine repentance, an acknowledgment of the need to be obedient to Christ and a heartfelt commitment to do so, but the outworking in our lives can often take somewhat longer. For those who have already transitioned, the journey to live in line with their sex will likely be a long and painful one. For those living with acute gender dysphoria, it may take time to wrestle with and accept what God says, and they may feel that some temporary steps to lessen their dysphoria (*eg* the use of gender-neutral pronouns) are necessary while they are working this through. For those walking alongside, we must learn to be patient and to be there for the long haul.

A Christian response cannot stop here, however. If the consequence of our head response will be to leave some people with the potential for an ongoing, even lifelong, battle with intense suffering, we must also offer a hope response.

Discussion Questions

- How can churches help people to understand and enjoy the given nature of their identity as a man or a woman?
- How would you respond to a transgender person who wants to serve in your church? Can you think of parallel situations that might help you to handle this situation in a right and fair way?

4

A Hope Response

If the experience of those who live with gender dysphoria is primarily an issue of suffering rather than identity, how should we respond?

As Christians we are uniquely equipped to handle suffering well, and to help others to do the same. The best thing we can offer to those who are suffering is the gospel of Jesus Christ. It is through the gospel and through participation in its blessings that we can be equipped to endure when suffering is a prominent feature of our daily lives. The ultimate hope response for those who are transgender is found in the gospel.

Suffering and the Story of the Bible

The Bible is wonderfully practical when it addresses the topic of suffering. While there is little to explain why God allows suffering, there is much to help us navigate the reality of living amidst suffering. Much of this is found in the big story told through the books of the Bible.

The 66 books of the Bible join together to tell one story. It is the story of God, the story of his creation and the story of his people. We live as part of this story.

God's story starts with creation. As an act and overflow of his love, God creates everything. Humans are the pinnacle of this creation. When God creates, everything is declared 'very good' (Gen 1.31). At this point, everything is as it should be, everything works right and there is no pain and no suffering.

Sadly, this perfection does not last. Humans soon rebel against God (Genesis 3). Ultimately, we fail to trust God and to believe that what he says is best for us—we sin. As Adam and Eve eat from the one tree from which they were told not to eat, trusting the serpent rather than God, God's good creation becomes damaged and disrupted. Brokenness, pain and suffering enter the world, and every one of us who has been born since has experienced this brokenness in our bodies, our minds and in the world around us. We now live in a world where there are things which are not as they should be.

But in his love and mercy, God was not happy to abandon humanity to the mess we had created. From the earliest stages of the story, he made promises that he would deal with the evil that had started this problem (Gen 3.15). He was faithful to this promise, even when humans continued to be unfaithful, so much so that he gave up his own son to enact restoration. The problem which brought brokenness into the world was sin—a lack of trust in God. Jesus comes and lives a life of perfect trust in God. He dies as a substitute for sinners who should die, is raised back to life and ascends to be once again with God the Father. In all this, he defeats sin and disarms the great enemy of humanity.

The story ends with a scene yet to come. Jesus returns, bringing with him a new creation. He applies in full the victory he has won in his death and resurrection, and everything that is broken is put to rights. Every bit of suffering ceases. Every experience of pain comes to an end. And God himself wipes away our tears (Rev 21.4).

This story—the true story of the past, the present and the future—is a powerful resource to help us to navigate suffering.

The story helps us to understand that *we should expect suffering*. It does not tell us why God allows suffering, but it does tell us that suffering will be a regular part of life until Jesus returns and the new creation comes. The fact that some people will, in this lifetime, live with pain and suffering in relation to their gender identity should not be a surprise. All of us will live with pain and suffering of many different types in this life.

But the story also helps us see that *we should lament over suffering*. It does not just show us that suffering should be expected, as if that fact should enable us to get over it. The story shows us that suffering is to be expected, and yet suffering is not how things were meant to be. We were made to live in the very good, but now we live in the very-good-but-damaged. Deep down we all know this. We all know, not only that there is suffering, but that suffering should not exist. The Bible's story is uniquely able to explain why some things are not as they should be. How can it be wrong to transition when it feels so natural for someone with gender dysphoria? Because some things are not as they should be. Every one of us experiences this in different ways.

We should lament over suffering

This dissonance between what is and what should be gives us reason to lament. To lament is to express our deep experience of pain, sorrow or loss and, specifically, to express it to God. If suffering was just how things are meant to be, lamenting would be illogical. But in a story where suffering is never how things were meant to be, lamenting is the right and natural response. This is why so many of the psalms are laments. They are the right human response to the experience of suffering that should not be. And lamenting is powerful. It does not necessarily change our situation, but it does change us. So often, through our lamenting, God gives us the strength to keep walking through the pain.

Finally, the story shows us *we can have hope even in the face of suffering*. Whatever we experience, however great the pain, however acute our experience of brokenness, there is always reason to hope because we know the end of the story. There is a day when all pain will end. There is a day when all that is broken will be put to rights. There is a day when God himself will wipe away our tears. That day is not yet, but it is coming. We can wait with certain hope, knowing that however impossible it might seem at the moment, the glory we experience then will far outweigh any suffering we experience now (Rom 8.18; 2 Cor 4.17). Like a traveller who is enabled to endure an arduous journey because of the promise of the destination, we find the strength to endure our suffering by setting our minds on our eternal destination.

Suffering in Relationship

Another way that God equips us to handle suffering is through relationship. Though suffering is to be expected in this age, it is not something we are meant to face alone.

The first and most important relationship that is available to help us to endure suffering is relationship with God. One of the wonders of the Christian gospel is that we are not left to navigate this life alone. Our union with God is not only a future prospect; it starts in the here and now.

For every believer in Christ, the God of all comfort comes to make his dwelling place within us, and his promise to us is that 'As we share abundantly in Christ's sufferings, so through Christ we share abundantly in comfort too' (2 Cor 1.5). By his Holy Spirit, God lives inside of us, comforting, strengthening and even praying for us (Rom 8.26).

An intimate relationship with God is vital to navigating life

For all believers, at all times, an intimate relationship with God, developed and sustained through spiritual disciplines and committed participation in a local church, is vital to navigating life. This becomes only more true when we are in a situation of pain and suffering.

Also important are relationships with other Christians in the context of the church. God has not asked us to follow Jesus on our own, but as part of a family, the church. As those who have been adopted as God's children, Christian believers are family. It is part of who we are. But it also needs to be part of how we live. It is very possible to be family without living as family. The church should be a family where every person can be loved, supported and cared for. This experience of church family is vital for all believers but can take on an extra level of importance when we are facing pain and suffering.

Supporting the Suffering

How can we support those who are suffering? Often the best place to start is by listening. Listening is loving. It affirms the value of the individual who is suffering and shows that their experience is legitimate and that they are loved in the midst of it. Many who are suffering also find that having the opportunity to talk about their experience helps them.

We should then be very careful what we say in response. Since the Bible rarely gives indications as to the causes of specific suffering and since it does not give us guidance on how to discern causes, we should avoid trying to comfort people by offering explanations. Often the best initial response is just to acknowledge people's pain, express our sorrow over it and, if it is suffering which we have not experienced, acknowledge the limitations of our ability to understand it. 'I can't imagine what that must be like. I'm so sorry that this is so painful for you.' While we may feel such statements offer little, in the midst of great pain and suffering, they can actually be powerful words of comfort, legitimizing the pain, giving the person we are supporting a freedom to accept and to express what they feel, and taking away the sense of isolation that can come with suffering, and which can make it so much more painful.

We can also support those who are suffering by reminding them of the truths of God's story. We can point people back to the cross where the love of God for us is decisively demonstrated. The Father's willing sacrifice of his son to the intense suffering of the cross and the Son's obedient submission to the Father's plan of suffering, is the proof that whatever might happen to us, God loves us, and he knows what it is to suffer. We can also point people forward to the day when all pain and suffering end, when everything that has been broken is put to rights, and when God himself wipes away our tears.

Often, the ways we can be a good support to those who are suffering are the same as the ways we can seek to be a good friend. We can be the friend whom someone knows they can call when it is all getting too much. We can be the friend who can express our love by simply being present, even when there may be few words that seem to help. Sometimes we will need to be the friend who encourages someone to seek further help if their experience is having a significant impact on their mental health. In lots of practical, and often relatively simple ways, we can be friends who bring comfort and hope.[13]

God's Gift to the Church

It may also be that those who live with gender dysphoria are a gift from God to the church. Such brothers and sisters may be ideally placed to teach others of us what it looks like to follow Jesus.

Jesus' invitation to follow him was an invitation to a life of self-sacrifice which would often feel like death (Mark 8.34–35). Those who seek to follow Jesus faithfully while living out their sex in the midst of experiencing gender dysphoria are a beautiful example of the sort of costly self-sacrifice to which Jesus calls us all. They can be a powerful challenge and encouragement to us all to be radical in the way we follow Jesus.

It is also the case that those who live with ongoing suffering often have a much more keen excitement about the end of God's story. Their longing for the fulfilment of God's promise to wipe away our tears can be a challenge and inspiration to those of us who might find it easy to become comfortable in this life and to overlook the reality of brokenness in our own lives and in the world around us. Those who suffer in faithfulness to Jesus can help all of us to grow in our longing for the life to come and to pray 'Come, Lord Jesus!' (Rev 22.20).

Seeking to follow Jesus faithfully as someone who experiences gender dysphoria will not be easy, but God has provided us with the resources to persevere in this life when things are not easy. If we want to make a truly Christian response to transgender, we must take seriously the real-life experience of living with gender dysphoria, and we must seek to mediate the comfort and hope that can be found in the Bible's response to suffering.

Discussion Questions

- What can you do to be a better friend to those around you who are suffering?
- How can we effectively communicate the hope that the Bible's big story offers to those experiencing the pain of gender dysphoria?

5 Conclusion

A Christian response to transgender must start from the recognition that transgender is about real people and real-life experiences. While there are plenty of debates and discussions related to the topic, many of which are important, behind these debates are people, and a Christian response starts first and foremost by considering these real people.

A Christian response to transgender must include three elements. It starts with a heart response of love towards those who identify as transgender, and compassion towards those who experience the pain of gender dysphoria. In responding this way, we are following the example of Jesus who demonstrated God's love towards all people, and also exemplified the compassion which he calls us to show to others.

The right heart attitude is vital but must also be accompanied by the right way of thinking about transgender experience. We need a head response. While transgender is often thought to be an identity issue, the form of identity on which such a view relies—internal identity—faces several problems. Far better is divine identity, an identity given to us, rather than discovered within or achieved through our actions. Our identity as either a man or a woman is given to us by God and is therefore stable and static. We do not have to act in a certain way to be a man or a woman; we are a man or a woman because of how God has made us. This gives us the freedom to express our personality, likes and dislikes, without changing our identity as a man or woman. All of this means that transitioning to live in line with experienced gender is not the right or best response to the experience of gender dysphoria.

Those who experience gender dysphoria and follow Jesus are a gift from God to the church

If transitioning is not the answer to gender dysphoria, what can we offer to those who experience the pain that it can bring? This is where we must include a hope response. As Christians, we are uniquely equipped to handle suffering well, and to help others to do the same. The gospel is God's great offering to us in the face of suffering. God's story, told in the Bible, helps us to see that we are to expect suffering in this life, but also that we are to lament over suffering, and that we can have real hope. Suffering can also be faced through the sustaining power and encouragement of relationship with God and others in the context of church family. It may also be the case that those who experience gender dysphoria and come to follow Jesus are a gift from God to the church, a reminder and inspiration for what it looks like to be a true disciple of Jesus and to live in eager anticipation of his return and the age to come.

All three of these elements are necessary for a Christian response. To remove any one of them is to fail truly to respond in a Christ-like way, and to fail truly to love people. Most of us will find that one or two of the elements come most naturally to us. This can make it easy for us to default to an imbalanced response. To respond well, we must be deliberate about including all three elements.

The response outlined in this booklet leaves many questions unanswered and many specific situations overlooked, but the three-part structure can be employed to discern a Christian response to the many different questions and situations of which we may become aware.

This booklet opened with the observation that behind the debates related to transgender are real people. People, not pronouns, is the first and most important thing we must remember. The response of some Christians to transgender so far has sadly left some people believing the opposite to be true. Many people believe that for God, it is about pronouns, not people. Against that backdrop, we have an opportunity. An opportunity to show our love towards transgender people, but much more than that, an opportunity to show God's love.

Recommended Resources

P Sprinkle, *Embodied: Transgender Identities, the Church, and What the Bible Has to Say* (Colorado Springs, CO: David C Cook, 2021). The best Christian treatment of the topic.

A T Walker, *God and the Transgender Debate* (Epsom: The Good Book Company, 2017). A good treatment of the key questions, including a useful chapter on talking to children and teens.

M A Yarhouse, *Understanding Gender Dysphoria* (Downers Grove, IL: IVP, 2015). A useful perspective from a Christian clinical psychologist.

N R Pearcey, *Love Thy Body: Answering Hard Questions about Life and Sexuality* (Grand Rapids, MI: Baker Books, 2018). A look at our culture's rejection of the body, with a very helpful chapter on transgender.

Notes

1 'Glossary of Terms' (https://www.stonewall.org.uk/help-advice/glossary-terms). Accessed 15 April 2020.

2 For more on the diverse range of experiences of gender identity see M A Yarhouse and J Sadusky, *Approaching Gender Dysphoria* (Grove Ethics booklet E188) pp 10–12 and M A Yarhouse and J Sadusky, *Emerging Gender Identities* (Grand Rapids, MI: Brazos, 2020).

3 For example, World Professional Association for Transgender Health, *Standards for Care for the Health of Transsexual, Transgender, and Gender Nonconforming People*, 7th version (WPATH: https://www.wpath.org/publications/soc, 2012) p 16. However, dissenting voices are emerging, *eg*, R D'Angelo *et al*, 'One Size Does Not Fit All: In Support of Psychotherapy for Gender Dysphoria,' *Archives of Sexual Behavior* (2020).

4 Names have been changed but both stories are true.

5 J Sabia-Tanis, 'Holy Creation, Wholly Creative' in J K Beilby and P R Eddy (eds), *Understanding Transgender Identities* (Grand Rapids, MI: Baker Academic, 2019) pp 209–210.

6 The word translated 'mercy' in Luke 10.37 is *eleos* but in context is clearly parallel to the use of *splanchnizomai* in 10.33.

7 Katy Steinmetz, 'Caitlyn Jenner on Privilege, Reality TV and Deciding to Come Out,' *Time*, 9 December 2015 (https://time.com/4142000/time-person-of-the-year-runner-up-caitlyn-jenner-interview/). Accessed 22 April 2020. Emphasis added.

8 Though it is often assumed that the image is damaged or lost through sin, this is never explicitly stated in Scripture and post-fall references to the image imply that it is still intact (*eg* Gen 5.1–3; 9.6; 1 Cor 11.7; Jas 3.9). See John F Kilner, 'Humanity in God's Image: Is the Image Really Damaged?' *Journal of the Evangelical Theological Society* 53/3 (Sept 2010) pp 601–617.

9 L Mayer and P McHugh, 'Sexuality and Gender: Findings from the Biological, Psychological, and Social Sciences,' *The New Atlantis* 50 (2016) pp 10–143: 'There is no other widely accepted biological classification for the sexes' (p 90).

10 See P Sprinkle, 'A Biblical Conversation About Transgender Identities,' Pastoral Paper 12, *The Center for Faith, Sexuality and Gender* (https://www.centerforfaith.com/resources).

11 Some make the claim that transgender people have a brain that is differently sexed to their reproductive system (brain sex theory). There are elements of the brain that are often different between males and females, but these differences are often present, not always. The reproductive system remains the only solid binary on which an identification as male or female can be made. See further P Sprinkle, 'Sex, Gender, and Transgender Experiences: Part 4—Brain Sex Theory,' *The Center for Faith and Sexuality* (https://centerforfaith.com/blog/sex-gender-and-transgender-experiences-part-4-brain-sex-theory).

12 There are few reliable studies on the long-term outcomes of transitioning, but recent studies suggest that transitioning often does not improve mental health outcomes. See M Konrad and K Kostev, 'Increased prevalence of depression, anxiety, and adjustment and somatoform disorders in transsexual individuals,' *Journal of Affective Disorders* 274 (Sept 2020) pp 482–485; and 'Correction to Bränström and Pachankis,' *American Journal of Psychiatry* 177/8 (Aug 2020) p 734. There are also growing calls for research into whether psychotherapy may be a better way to respond to gender dysphoria. See, for example, R D'Angelo *et al*, 'One Size Does Not Fit All: In Support of Psychotherapy for Gender Dysphoria,' *Archives of Sexual Behavior* (2020).

13 It is also worth noting that some detransitioners have shared strategies to help others living with gender dysphoria. For example, Nele Peer Jongeling and Elie Vandenbussche, 'Gender Detransition: A Path Towards Self-Acceptance,' pp 40–46 (https://post-trans.com/detransition-booklet).